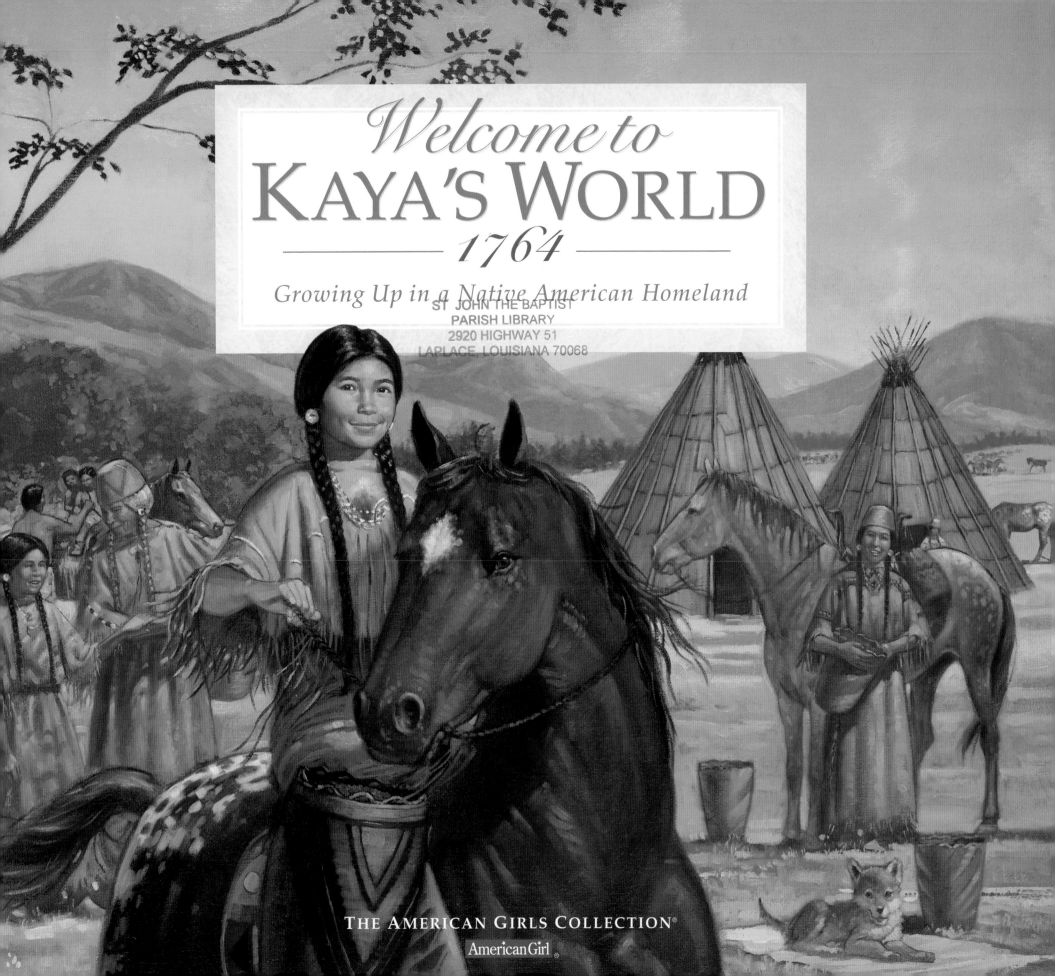

Welcome to
KAYA'S WORLD
— *1764* —

Growing Up in a Native American Homeland

THE AMERICAN GIRLS COLLECTION®

American Girl®

Published by Pleasant Company Publications
Copyright © 2003 by Pleasant Company
For information, address: Book Editor,
Pleasant Company Publications,
8400 Fairway Place, P.O. Box 620998,
Middleton, WI 53562.

Visit our Web site at **americangirl.com**

Printed in China
03 04 05 06 07 08 LEO 10 9 8 7 6 5 4 3 2 1
The American Girls Collection®, Kaya®, and the
American Girl logo are trademarks of Pleasant Company.

Written by Dottie Raymer
Edited by Jodi Evert
Designed and Art Directed by Will Capallero, Lara Klipsch Elliott, and Jane S. Varda
Produced by Cheryll Mellenthin, Paula Moon, Mary Cudnohfsky, Jeannette Bailey
Cover Illustration by Bill Farnsworth
Interior Illustrations by Bill Farnsworth, Laszlo Kubini, Susan McAliley, Susan Moore,
Justin Packard, and Jean-Paul Tibbles
Illustration and Image Research by Kathy Borkowski and Sally Jacobs
Photography by Jamie Young and Radlund Photography
Prop Research and Styling by Jean doPico
Permissions Coordination by Gail Longworth

Library of Congress Cataloging-in-Publication Data
Available upon request.

GLOSSARY OF NEZ PERCE WORDS

In *Welcome to Kaya's World*, Nez Perce words are spelled so that English readers
can pronounce them. Here, you can also see how the words are actually
spelled and said by the Nez Perce people.

Phonetic/Nez Perce	Pronunciation	Meaning
ah-la-tah-mal/alatama'l	*ah-lah-tah-MAHL*	the season when it is difficult to build fires because fuel is scarce
ah-pah-al/apa'al	*ah-pah-AHL*	the season for making loaves from the kouse root
ha-oo-koy/haoq'qy	*HA-oo-khoy*	the season when new life begins in deer and elk
ha-soo-al/hesu'al	*ha-soo-AHL*	the season when eels run in the streams
Hah-hahts	*HAH-hahts*	Grizzly Bear
heel-lal/hilal	*heel-LAHL*	the season of melting snow in the mountains
hope-lal/hoplal	*HOPE-lal*	the season when the tamarack trees lose their needles and trees change color
Hun-ya-wat/Hanyaw'áat	*hun-yah-WAHT*	the Creator
Kaya'aton'my'	*ky-YAAH-a-ton-my*	she who arranges rocks
keh-kee-tal/q'eq'iitt'al	*keh-khee-TAHL*	the season for the first harvest of roots
koy-sal/qoyxt'sal	*khoy-TSAHL*	the season when blueback salmon run in the streams
lah-te-tal/latit'al	*lah-TEE-tahl*	the season of new plants and flowers beginning to blossom
Nimíipuu	*nee-MEE-poo*	The People; known today as the Nez Perce Indians
pe-koon-my-kal/piq'uunm'ayq'al	*pe-khoon-my-KAHL*	the season when the fall salmon run upstream and the fingerlings journey down the river
sek-le-wáal/sexliwetés	*sehk-le-WAHL*	the season when trees drop their leaves and cold comes to the high country
ta-ya-al/taya'al	*TAH-yah-ahl*	the season of midsummer hot weather
tah-seeh	*TAH-seeh*	a giant, hairy animal related to the woolly mammoth
tee-kas/tikée's	*tee-KAHS*	baby board, or cradleboard
toos-te-ma-sa-tal/tuustimasat'al	*toose-te-mah-SAH-tahl*	the season for traveling to the high country to dig roots
wa-wama-aye-khal/waw' ama' ayqáal	*wah-wah-mah-eye-KHAL*	the season when Chinook salmon reach the canyon streams
we-lu-poop/wilupup	*we-LUH-poop*	the season when cold air travels
wyakin/wéeyekin	*WHY-ah-kin*	guardian spirit

Table of Contents

Welcome to Kaya's World

From the book *Changes for Kaya*

"Kaya's heart swelled. She felt how strongly she loved her beautiful homeland and all the creatures that shared it with Nimíipuu."

— Janet Shaw,
Changes for Kaya

From the back of her beloved horse, Steps High, Kaya could see the sheltering peaks of the Bitterroot Mountains before her. She could hear the rushing waters of the river and the splashing of the salmon who offered themselves as food for her people. She could smell the familiar scents of smoke from the tepee fires and feel a quiver of delight run along her horse's back. Kaya felt the same quiver run through her own body. Surely the stories of the elders were true—Coyote had, indeed, chosen the most beautiful place on earth for her people, *Nimíipuu*. Here in this valley, the earth, their mother, provided everything they needed— everything they would ever need.

Kaya knew, too, that even the earth brought change. She knew that when the snows moved across the mountains, she and her family would move, too, just as they always had done, following the seasons to gather their food. Already change had come to her people. Beside the longhouse fire, Kaya's grandmother told stories of a time before horses, and the changes the horses had brought. Some of the changes were good ones—swift travel, good food supplies, new friends and trade. But there were bad changes, too—deadly diseases, enemy raids, war.

Kaya's grandmother hinted at an even greater change as well—change brought by strangers with pale faces from far away. For Kaya, these changes were no more than whispers in the wind. She knew that if she did her best to be a good Nimíipuu, she would have the strength and spirit to survive whatever came her way.

w COYOTE CREATED NIMÍIPUU

*According to Nimíipuu legend, animals lived on earth long before
here were any human beings. One of these animals was a smart but
ricky character named Coyote. In Kaya's time, elders told this legend
of how Coyote created Nimíipuu, and they still tell it today.*

Long ago, when animals could talk and act like people, a
terrible monster came and began to eat up all the animals.
Coyote was lonely without the other animals around, so he
decided he would stop the monster.

Coyote got three pieces of rope and a bone knife. He tied
himself to three mountains—Cottonwood Butte, Seven Devils
Mountain, and Pilot Knob. Then he shouted to the monster,
"Monster! You have swallowed my brothers and sisters. Now
swallow me!" The monster tried three times to swallow Coyote,
but each time the mountains stopped him.

Coyote used his knife to cut the ropes and allowed himself to
be swallowed. Once inside the monster, he met up with Grizzly
Bear, who rose up and growled at him. Coyote said, "You growl
at me, but you weren't so fierce when the monster swallowed
you!" And he kicked the bear in the nose. That is why grizzly
bears have flat noses.

The next animal Coyote met was Rattlesnake, who rattled
and hissed at him. "You rattle at me, but you weren't so fierce
when the monster swallowed you!" And Coyote stomped on
Rattlesnake's head. That is why rattlesnakes have flat heads.

Coyote reached the monster's stomach, where he built a
great fire. With his knife he began to cut out the monster's heart.
Finally, the monster died, and the animals escaped. Coyote
cut the monster into pieces and threw them far to the east, west,
north, and south. Wherever a piece landed, a different group
of humans sprang up. Some were tall and warlike. Others were
small, but good fishermen.

Then Coyote's brother Fox said, "Coyote, look at this
beautiful valley. Why didn't you put any people here?" Coyote
took some of the monster's blood and sprinkled it on the ground.
He said, "This place is for The People, Nimíipuu. They will be
strong and brave, and they will make a good life in this valley."
And so, the Nimíipuu nation was born.

Ancient Homelands

Kaya began each day with a prayer of thanks to *Hun-ya-wat*, the Creator, for the earth, the sky, the water, and all the living things around her. Kaya's people believed that their spirits were part of the land—a land of rugged peaks and deep canyons, dense forests and vast grasslands, gently rolling hills and swift-moving rivers. For thousands of years, Kaya's people had taken care of the land, and it had given them everything they needed to survive and grow strong.

LEGENDARY MAMMOTHS
According to Nez Perce legend, their people once hunted a giant, hairy animal called the *tah-seeh*. The tah-seeh might have been related to the woolly mammoth of prehistoric times.

A FRENCH NAME
Nimíipuu are known today as the Nez Perce (nez purse). The name means "pierced nose" in French. It was given to Nimíipuu by white explorers who mistook Nimíipuu for a tribe who wore shells through their noses.

NEZ PERCE HOMELAND
In Kaya's time, the Nez Perces' home-land, shown on the map in red, covered about 27,000 square miles of modern-day Idaho, Washington, and Oregon.

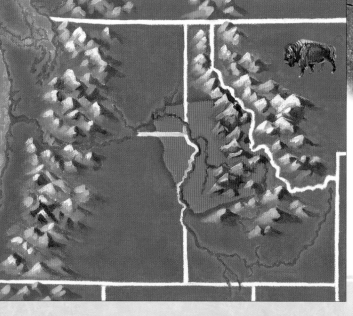

PREHISTORIC PETROGLYPHS
Ancient pictures carved in rock, called petroglyphs (PET-roh-gliffs), have been found in Nez Perce homelands. The petroglyphs prove that people have lived in the area for more than 11,000 years.

HEART OF THE MONSTER
The Heart of the Monster
landmark, where Coyote
is said to have created
the Nez Perce people,
has stood in Nez Perce
country for thousands
of years. You can find
it today in the Nez Perce
National Park in the
Kamiah Valley in Idaho.

Coyote's Fishnet

Children like Kaya listened carefully
when their elders told them stories
about Coyote and other animals. These
stories taught them lessons about the
world around them and
how to survive and live
together. Sometimes leg-
ends told about important
landmarks. This legend
tells about a special rock
formation near the
Clearwater River.

One day Coyote was fishing with
his net in the river. Black Bear came
along and told him, "Why are you still
here? The fish are all gone. You should
be helping the people hunt for buffalo."

Coyote knew that Black Bear was
right, but he didn't want to admit it.
"There are plenty of fish here," he said.
"I will catch them soon enough."

"No you won't," said Black Bear.

"Yes I will!" shouted Coyote, and
the two began to argue. Finally, Coyote
got so mad that he flung his fishnet up
into the hills. He grabbed Black Bear,
threw him across the river, and turned
him to stone. "That will teach you
not to poke your nose into other
people's business!" he cried. And he
stalked away in a huff.

Horse People

Kaya's grandmother told her, "When I was a girl, we didn't even *have* horses." When Kaya was a girl, horses had been part of Nez Perce life for only fifty years.

According to tradition, the Nez Perce first saw horses while visiting their friends, the Cayuses, who had traded for them with their southern neighbors, the Shoshones. The Nez Perces immediately sent an expedition to trade for horses of their own. The Nez Perce valleys turned out to be ideal for raising horses, and the Nez Perce people soon became known for their swift horses and fine horsemanship.

HEAVY LOADS
Horses allowed Nez Perces to travel farther and faster and to carry more goods. The Nez Perces packed heavy loads onto a wooden structure called a *travois* (trah-VOY). A travois was made from two long poles lashed to either side of a horse.

THE WHITE MARE
One of the first horses Nez Perces received was a beautiful white mare like this one. According to legend, all of the Nez Perce herds descended from that mare and her foal.

THE NEZ PERCE HORSE
Nez Perces knew how to breed horses that were the perfect mix of speed, endurance, strength, and surefootedness. Oftentimes, the horses had unusual spotted markings, too. The Nez Perces didn't breed for spots, but spotted horses became known as the "Nez Perce Horse," or Appaloosa.

The name "Appaloosa" comes from the name of the Nez Perce horses' summer grazing land, near the Palouse (pah-LOOSE) River.

Ceremonies

Horses became an important part of Nez Perce ceremonies, such as parades to honor ancestors or to prepare for battle. In battle, warriors' lives often depended on their swift, nimble mounts.

Small groups of women rode for days to gather food for their families and villages. Horses made this important job faster and easier.

Valuable Possessions

Horses were a sign of wealth. Some bands of Nez Perces kept herds of more than a thousand horses. Most families owned between ten and twenty-five horses, although some had as many as several hundred.

The New Nez Perce Horse

The first horses that came to the North American west arrived with the Spaniards in the early 1500s. These horses were light-bodied, were very fast, and could run long distances.

The Nez Perces bred descendants of these horses for sturdiness and surefootedness—qualities that horses needed on steep mountain trails. At the same time, the Nez Perces kept the qualities of slimness, speed, and endurance. This skillful breeding created a horse that made the Nez Perce famous.

In the 1800s, pioneers brought more powerful, wagon-pulling horses that crossed with the Nez Perce horses. Slowly, the qualities of slimness and speed, part of what made Nez Perce horses so prized, were lost.

Today, the Nez Perce have crossed the dramatically spotted, sturdy Appaloosa with the swift, elegant Akhal-Teke (AH-kahl TEH-kee), a rare desert horse from Asia, to re-create the original Nez Perce Horse.

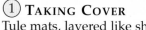

On The Move

The Nez Perces traveled with the seasons and built different types of homes for summer and winter. While traveling during the summer, they built small tepees covered with mats made from tule (TOO-lee) reeds. Each tepee housed one extended family— mother, father, children, grandparents, and visiting relatives. When it was time to move camp, the women took down the poles and rolled up the mats to carry with them to the next campsite— the perfect mobile home!

① **TAKING COVER**
Tule mats, layered like shingles, were the perfect all-weather covering. In wet weather, the reeds swelled to keep out rain. In dry weather, the reeds allowed breezes to blow through. The mats could also be rolled up in hot weather.

④ **PLAY TEPEES**
Girls practiced building their own play-sized tepees. Play tepees were important practice—women were responsible for building their families' homes.

④

② FRAME IT

Women used pine poles to make the frame of the tepee. They leaned four poles against one another and tied them together at the top. Then they leaned the other poles against the first poles to make a cone shape.

③ COZY COMFORT

Families kept their belongings along the walls of the tepee. They built a fire in the middle for cooking and heat. The smoke from the fire escaped through a hole at the top of the tepee.

9

Life in the Longhouse

When snow began to fall in the high country, most Nez Perce families returned to their permanent villages in the protected canyons. There, they cooked and slept in long, mat-covered houses. Each longhouse was home to several families—and sometimes the entire village!

Dressed in warm hides, girls and boys helped their relatives prepare food and make clothes, baskets, and weapons. As they worked, they listened to the legends and stories their elders told. Over time, they learned the stories by heart and repeated them to their children, and their children's children.

① EXTRA PROTECTION
Like tepees, longhouses were built with poles covered with tule mats. Extra poles were propped against the mats on the outside to keep them from blowing away.

② ENTRANCES AND EXITS
Family members entered the longhouse through small openings in the wall along one side of the lodge. Heavy buffalo hides hung from the top of each opening to keep out the chilly winter winds.

③ OUTDOOR CHORES
Even in the bitter cold, people still had outdoor chores to do. Women collected firewood and water from nearby streams. Men hunted deer, elk, and smaller game on horseback or sometimes on snowshoes.

④ INSULATION
Hide liners hung from the lodge poles to keep out cold winds. In addition, rolled-up hides were stacked along the inside walls.

⑤ STORAGE ROOM
Dried fish, camas-root cakes, and other preserved foods were stored in baskets and bags along the walls. Each family had its own store of food, but all village members were quick to share if supplies ran low.

⑪ A Little Light

A slit running along the top of the longhouse allowed smoke to go out and a bit of daylight to come in. At night, people did their work by flickering firelight.

⑩ Cozy Beds

Family members slept on beds made of dry grasses and the inner bark of cottonwood trees. For pillows, they used rolled mats or hide bags stuffed with cattail fluff. Blankets made from buffalo hides kept them toasty warm.

⑨ Closets

Valuable clothing was hung from the poles that made the walls of the lodge. Other clothing was stored in baskets or in rawhide envelopes called *parfleches*.

⑧ Winter Work

Women made and mended clothes and wove baskets during the winter months, when they weren't busy gathering foods. Men used the time to make horsehair ropes, spears and nets for fishing, or bows and arrows for hunting.

⑥ Dug In

Longhouse floors were built below ground level. People piled the dirt from digging out the foundation around the outside walls for extra warmth.

⑦ Friendly Fires

Usually, two families shared a fire and kept it burning day and night. Children knew that Whipwoman would hear about it if they let the fire go out!

A New Baby

The birth of a child was a welcome event in a Nez Perce village. About a month or two before a baby was born, the mother moved to a small, separate birthing lodge. During this time, she spoke and ate only with female relatives, who brought her food and instructed her on childbirth and infant care. As soon as the child was born, the village crier announced the birth to the rest of the community. Relatives brought gifts and celebrated with feasts for the mother and baby, and all gave thanks for the new life.

SAFE AND SOUND
A cradleboard, or *tee-kas*, kept a baby safe and snug until he or she was ready to walk. Nez Perce parents believed that cradleboards gave children straight backs and legs and strong spirits.

A rosewood hoop protected the baby's head if the cradleboard tipped or fell.

A buckskin or woven hood shaded the baby's head in summer and kept it warm in winter.

Nez Perce women used paints, porcupine quills, and beads to decorate cradleboards with colorful designs.

SLEEP, BABY, SLEEP
Cradleboards allowed mothers to use their hands while keeping babies close by. Mothers could wear the cradleboards on their backs, prop them against a tree trunk, or hang them on a saddle. Often the rocking motion of a walking horse would lull the baby to sleep.

Many people believed that the birth of twins brought good luck to the family and that the twins themselves would have good luck throughout their lives.

Many Names

The name a Nez Perce baby was given at birth was just one of the names she received throughout her life. Kaya's mother named her daughter for the first thing she saw after giving birth—a woman arranging stones for a sweat lodge. She hoped the name— *Kaya'aton'my'*—would give Kaya the woman's strength and wisdom.

As they grew up, children often received the names of ancestors at special naming ceremonies. As they got older, they often received other names that described special skills or important deeds. The Nez Perces believed that no one could use the name of another person unless the owner chose to give it away, as Swan Circling gave her name to Kaya. Most children received their most important names at age 12 or 13, after they went on their vision quests to seek guardian spirits. Later, at a sacred dance ceremony, the child would reveal the spirit's name and have the honor of taking it as her or his own.

A PEA IN A POD
At night, babies swung in cradles that looked like buckskin hammocks. The edges of the cradle were gathered to keep the baby snug and warm.

A soft buckskin covering and laces held the baby securely in place.

Soft moss or cattail fluff tucked in the bottom of the cradleboard served as a natural diaper.

Baby moccasins

SILENCE IS GOLDEN
By the time Nez Perce babies were ready to leave the cradleboards, they already knew the importance of being quiet and obedient. Crying could scare away game or, even worse, attract wild animals or enemies.

Play with a Purpose

Nez Perce children grew up under the watchful eyes of a large, loving family. Brothers, sisters, and cousins all played together and looked after one another. Young children spent lots of time outdoors exploring the woods, streams, and prairies around them. Handmade toys and games kept them entertained while others worked, and gave them practice in the skills they'd need later in life.

PLAYMATES AND PROTECTORS
Village dogs were loving playmates and loyal protectors. Their keen sense of smell enabled them to warn the village of predators before they could be seen.

TENDER LOVING CARE
Girls in Kaya's time loved their dolls as dearly as girls do today. They tucked their dolls into miniature cradleboards and dressed them in carefully beaded buckskin dresses, just as real mothers did.

HORSEPLAY
Stick horses gave children practice in caring for horses—and the chance to imagine themselves as warrior men and women!

PLAYING HOUSE
Setting up miniature tepees for their dolls gave girls a chance to practice the skills they would need to build their own homes when they were older.

DEER HOOF GAME
This game helped children sharpen their aim. Players held the wooden pin pointing up and let the deer hooves hang down. Then they swung the string and tried to catch the hooves on the pin.

PRACTICE PACKING
Small painted parfleches, or rawhide storage envelopes, held doll accessories and other tiny toys. When girls grew up, they learned how to pack large parfleches with all their family's belongings.

TOY CANOE
Children carved tiny toy canoes from branches or small trees. An adult-size canoe was 30 feet long and carved from a single tree.

THE POWER OF THE IMAGINATION
Children used their imaginations to make their own toys. One elder woman remembered making a miniature village out of stones and shells. She wrapped the stones in bits of deerskin to make people and used mussel shells for horses. Then she made tiny bows out of grass and placed them by the people to protect them as they slept.

Strong Minds and Bodies

Every morning, before the sun's first rays had even begun to peek over the mountains, elders roused the village's children from beneath their cozy deerskin blankets. Down to the river they'd run—in winter as well as summer—to bathe and swim. Children exercised constantly, running footraces, riding horses, and playing ball games. Girls took part in all these activities and were as skillful as the boys. All these lessons conditioned children's bodies and focused their minds.

LESSONS FOR LIFE
Grandparents, or elders, were the main teachers in the community because they had the most patience, wisdom, and experience. They taught children to have sharp memories. Everything in Nez Perce culture was passed on by example and through songs, stories, and legends that children learned by heart.

TAKE THE PLUNGE
The Nez Perces often built their sweat lodges next to streams so that bathers could plunge into cold water the minute they left their steamy bath. Nez Perces pushed heated rocks inside the sweat lodge, and then poured cold water over them to make steam.

GOOD SHOT!
Shooting games helped young warriors develop keen eyes and steady aim. In this game, players tried to throw long sticks through a rolling hoop while it was in motion. Older children played the game with bows and arrows.

SLIPPERY SPIN

In winter, children made a slippery game of spinning tops on the ice. The tops were made from stone or out of round, flat pieces of bark with pointed pegs stuck through their centers.

SWOOSH!

In wintertime, girls and boys used snowshoes to walk—and sometimes race!—through deep snow. They knew that speed and stamina were important for survival, but mostly they just loved to race.

SHINNY

Both children and adults played ball games. One game, known today as "shinny," used a curved stick and a leather ball filled with deer fur. Shinny was played like today's ice or field hockey.

A shinny stick and ball

Vision Quest

As children grew older, elders prepared them for the most important event in their lives—the vision quest. At the age of 12 or 13, each child went alone to an isolated place, perhaps deep in the woods or high on a mountaintop. The child ate no food and drank little water. If he or she prepared well, a *wyakin*, or spirit helper, would appear. The wyakin would grant the child its special powers—perhaps the swiftness of a deer or the courage of a mountain lion. After a child received a wyakin, that wyakin was always available to him or her. The identity of a person's wyakin was a private matter, revealed only at certain ceremonies and to close family and friends.

A Prized Possession

Nez Perce children grew up with horses. As infants, they rocked in cradleboards hung from saddle horns. As toddlers, they rode tied to the saddle behind older relatives on trails to hunting or root-gathering grounds. By the time they were nine or ten, children rode well, and they knew how to train and care for their horses. The Nez Perce people treated all horses with respect and honored their own with fine trappings.

Young girls helped make decorated horse trappings. Dangling shells jingled in time with the horse's trot. Small feathers or beads embellished bridles. Each horse was dressed as uniquely as the girl who rode it.

SADDLE
Women's saddles were made out of wood covered with rawhide and decorated with painted designs and fringe.

FOREHEAD FINERY
This beaded forehead ornament was probably a gift or trade item from the Crow people.

HORSEHAIR ROPE
Braided horsehair made fine, strong rope used for many things—including bridles and reins. Nez Perces twisted or braided different colors of hair to make the ropes beautiful as well as strong.

QUIRT
Riders used *quirts*, or horsewhips, to urge their horses forward while hunting or in battle. Antlers were used to make the handles, and strips of deer or buffalo hide were attached for the lashes.

To make stirrups, the Nez Perces heated strips of green wood and bent them into shape. As the strips cooled, the wood became very stiff and strong.

High horns, or pommels, made a perfect place to hang saddlebags and cradleboards.

HORSE COLLAR

Nez Perce girls learned how to weave beautiful designs into long collars that they draped around the necks of their horses.

PARADING WITH PRIDE

Today, as in Kaya's time, men, women, girls, and boys parade their horses in their finest regalia, or outfits, to show pride in Nez Perce artistry and culture.

Flowing saddlebag fringes hung nearly to the ground and swayed gracefully as the horse walked.

19

A World of Danger

Danger was always present in the Nez Perces' lives. A small fish harvest meant that food stores might not last through the winter. A harsh winter might put off the first root gatherings, leaving the village short of food during the early spring. Dry summers could spark devastating mountain fires. And always, enemy raiders and animal predators loomed just outside the safe confines of the village.

BEARS
Grizzly bears were respected and feared for their tremendous strength and fierceness. The courageous warrior who killed a bear had the privilege of wearing its claws on a necklace.

A CIRCLE OF PROTECTION
Nez Perces protected themselves against enemy raids by setting their tepees in a circle. At night, they drove the horse herds into the center of the circle, where the horses could be easily guarded.

FIRE!
In summer, lightning started grass fires that raced through the hot, dry canyons. Families counted on warnings from scouts to give them time to flee a fire's path of destruction.

RATTLESNAKES
Rattlesnakes lived along the steep trails of canyons. The Nez Perces used herbs to draw the poison out of rattlesnake bites.

A Spiritual Brother

Nez Perce children were taught that humans were the last—and therefore the youngest—creatures on earth. They learned to look to their elders, the animals, for wisdom and strength in the face of danger. From the wolf they learned to protect their young, to be quick and sure in hunting, and to use their wits to survive. People who had wolf wyakins, like Kaya's father, Toe-ta, were known for their strong hunting powers.

Today, people can learn more about wolves by visiting the Wolf Education Center in Winchester, Idaho. The Nez Perce tribe adopted a pack of wolves that were featured in the documentaries *Wolf: Return of a Legend* and *Wolves at Our Door*. Visitors can take a guided hike to see the 20-acre enclosure of wolves, if the wolves choose to be seen.

NATURAL MEDICINES

Medicine men and women, or healers, used herbs and other natural substances to cure illnesses. Sage helped relieve sneezes and sniffles, and juniper was boiled to make a disinfecting bath.

DREAD DISEASES

The pockmarks on Kaya's grandmother's face came from a disease called smallpox. White people brought this terrible disease. It killed hundreds of Nez Perces, and sometimes wiped out whole villages. Some people survived, but they were scarred for life.

MOUNTAIN LIONS

Girls like Kaya protected themselves by learning the ways of animals. Kaya knew that mountain lions felt threatened when someone stared into their eyes. If she met a mountain lion, she didn't look at it directly. She knew that a threatened mountain lion was more likely to pounce!

How Bear Helped Nimíipuu

Legends like this one about the grizzly bear taught children not to fear death and to respect the spiritual powers of their animal brothers and sisters.

Long ago, when the people were first on the earth and animals could still talk, a little boy strayed too far from his village. For days, the boy wandered lost, without food or water. Then one day, he came upon *Hah-hahts*, Grizzly Bear.

Now Hah-hahts had heard from his friend Coyote that Nimíipuu were coming to live on the land. Hah-hahts had never seen Nimíipuu, but he was sure he hated them. He thought Nimíipuu wanted to take away the land he loved.

Hah-hahts reared up on his hind legs and bared his sharp teeth and claws. "Child of Nimíipuu!" he growled. "Do you think you can take my land from me? I will tear you to pieces with one swipe of my paw!"

The boy just stood gazing at Hah-hahts. Finally he said in a quiet voice, "All you can do is kill me. I am not afraid of death. Death is only a part of life."

Hah-hahts stopped in his tracks. "All other animals fear me, but you do not!" he said. "You are as brave as me and as wise as Coyote. You must deserve to live on this land. Come with me. I will show you all you need to know about your new home."

Hah-hahts flipped the boy onto his back and carried him off into the high country. He showed the boy the streams where Salmon ran in the spring and the homes of Deer and Elk. He climbed along the backbone of the mountains and showed the boy the lands where Buffalo lived. He pointed out huckleberry and serviceberry bushes and the meadows where camas bulbs grew.

Finally, Hah-hahts took the boy back to his village. "Now you know all I know about this land," he said. "Go and tell your people that as long as Nimíipuu honor the land, it will be theirs to use."

Making a Match

In Kaya's time, young people usually were not the ones to decide whom they were going to marry. Parents arranged the marriages of their children. They had to be sure that the future husband or wife was an honorable person and a strong worker who would be able to provide for a family.

After both families agreed to a match, a female relative of the groom went to live with the bride's family. She would observe the girl to see if she would make a good wife. Later, the boy lived with the family so that they could make sure he was a good provider. If both young people proved themselves worthy of the match, the families set a date for a gift-giving ceremony to seal the marriage.

COURTSHIP DANCE
Girls and boys formed circles for courtship dances, with boys in the outside circle and girls in the inside circle. When a boy got close to the girl of his choice, he placed a stick on her shoulder. If the girl left the stick on her shoulder, she chose him, too!

COURTING
This photo shows a courting couple in 1903. In Kaya's time, some parents considered their sons' and daughters' choices!

A SWEET SERENADE
Young men serenaded their sweethearts by playing soft melodies on flutes outside the girls' tepees. They made their flutes by hollowing out stems from elderberry bushes.

WEDDING SPOONS
According to custom, the groom's family gave the bride the sheep's-horn spoons she used at her wedding feast.

THEY'RE OFF!
Horse racing and other contests of speed and skill were perfect opportunities for young men to impress their sweethearts!

MIXED MARRIAGES
In Kaya's time, marriage to a person in another tribe was good for trading, and it meant less warring and raiding, too. Brides dressed in the ceremonial style of their people. The bride above wears a head covering of shells, beads, and Chinese coins, a tradition of the Wishram and Yakama peoples.

THE GIVE-AWAY
During gift-giving ceremonies, members of the bride's family gave gifts that represented the bride's contributions to the family, such as baskets filled with roots and berries. The groom's family gave items that showed the young man's skills, such as animal hides or dried fish.

MAKING GIFTS
Brides-to-be made many beautiful gifts for their new families, such as the painted parfleche Brown Deer planned to give to Cut Cheek's mother.

Dresses from Deer

The clothes that Nez Perce girls wore, like everything else in their lives, came from the natural world around them. Girls sewed together deer, elk, or sheep hides to make long, fringed dresses. A well-made dress was a gift to the Creator and an honor to the woman or girl who made it.

④ PLANNING
It took two skins to make one dress—one skin for the back and one for the front. The hides were laid upside down so that the tails were at the top.

① SCRAPING
Women stretched hides on wooden frames to flatten them and prevent them from shrinking. They cleaned the inside of the skin with stone or bone scrapers.

② SOAKING
To remove the hair, women dusted the hides with wood ashes and soaked them in water. After a few days, the hair was loose enough to take off with scrapers made out of a deer or elk bone—and a lot of elbow grease!

③ TANNING
To tan the hides, women carefully rubbed a paste of crushed animal brains onto the skin. Then they smoked the hides to make them waterproof and durable.

⑤ MAKING SINEW

Women made sinew thread by separating the tendons of buffalo, elk, or other large animals. They licked the end of the thread and twisted it to make a sharp point. While they were working, they kept the rest of the sinew balled up in their mouths so that it stayed moist and flexible.

⑦ FINISHING TOUCH

To make the yoke, or top part of the dress, women folded the tail of the deer over and sewed it down. They left on the tail as a sign of respect for the deer.

Beaded awl case

⑥ LACING IT UP

Instead of needle and thread, women used a sharp tool called an awl to poke holes in the deerskin. Then they threaded sinew through the holes to lace the edges together.

One of a Kind

Young girls' clothes were usually plain and practical. But girls also spent hours decorating special outfits with elaborate patterns of quills, shells, and beads. Girls excitedly looked forward to the honor of wearing their beautiful dresses at a tribal ceremony or feast.

This dress, made in the mid-1800s, is decorated in the same style as a dress Kaya would have worn, but it has many more beads and shells than were available to her. In Kaya's time, women would have used colorful porcupine quills or painted designs to give their dresses unique style.

Women attached long ribbons of fringe by threading them through tiny slits in the dress and then knotting or beading the fringes to keep them in place.

An elk has only two teeth that are large enough to use for decoration. That made the teeth rare and much desired!

Dresses were fringed along the bottom, sleeves, and side seams. Fringes added grace to a woman's movements.

Women preferred to use the skins of female animals for dresses. They believed that an animal passed along qualities such as swiftness or bravery to the person who wore its skin.

Tribes along the Pacific coast harvested shellfish called dentalium for their valuable shells. Just a few strings of these white shells were valuable enough to buy a prized horse!

During Kaya's time, women used geometric shapes to decorate their clothing. As they traded goods and ideas with other tribes, they began to include flowers and animals in their designs as well.

Heavily beaded dresses could weigh as much as 30 pounds!

European glass beads, bits of copper, and shiny coins were prized trade items long before whites reached Nez Perce country. Women added these signs of wealth to traditional designs on dresses and shirts.

Traders from Russia introduced blue glass beads to North America. They traded with Pacific Coast tribes who in turn traded the valuable beads to the Nez Perce.

When a dress became worn out, beaded sections were sometimes carefully removed and used again on a new dress.

Adornments

The Nez Perces were, and still are, experts at turning everyday things from nature—bones, grasses, shells, teeth, quills, hooves, hides, furs, and feathers—into beautiful, meaningful adornments. Trade items such as beads, coins, and thimbles from other cultures added even more creative possibilities.

Strings of Russian blue glass beads were used as money and as necklaces.

HATS

Today, woven hats are worn by women only for special occasions and ceremonies. In Kaya's time, women wore them as everyday work hats. Most hats had zigzag designs woven into them. Sometimes women added beads, shells, or feathers tied to leather laces hanging from the top of the hat.

Nez Perce girls and women took pride in carrying bags with carefully crafted patterns.

BEAUTY AND PROTECTION

Women and men wore chokers and breastplates made of long bone beads for adornment and to prevent arrows from piercing them in battle.

These decorations, called rosettes, could be used on clothing, on hide robes, or sometimes on tepees.

QUILLWORK
Women flattened porcupine quills by soaking them and then pressing them between rocks. They sorted them by size and then dyed them with herbs or minerals.

HIGH-TOPS
These floral high-top moccasins were made for a man in the mid-1900s. High-tops helped protect men's ankles while they hunted. Women always wore high-tops for modesty.

HAIR FASHIONS
Both men and women wore their hair braided in two braids. For special occasions, people wrapped strips of otter fur around their braids.

ABALONE HAIR TIES
Women wore round abalone shells as hair ties or earrings. According to Nez Perce legend, the shining colors of abalone shells came from lightning that was brought to earth to become fire.

BELT BAG
Girls wore small woven bags fastened at their waists. Inside, they kept bits of dried salmon, huckleberries, or root cakes for a quick meal, or they carried tools such as awls, knives, or sinew.

The Art of Weaving

Nez Perce women were talented weavers. They made woven water containers, cooking pots, horse trappings, hats, and all shapes and sizes of baskets, wallets, and bags for gathering and storing food and other items. Other tribes and, later, white traders recognized the beauty and usefulness of these well-made items. By Kaya's time, Nez Perces were trading their weavings for buffalo hides, horses, and other precious goods.

BASKET HATS
Women used a special technique, called "wrapped twining," for weaving hats. Wrapped twining makes a design appear only on the outside of the hat.

WEAVING WISDOM
One of the first skills a Nez Perce girl learned from her grandmother was how to make a basket. Grandmothers watched carefully to see that girls' baskets were woven tightly. The more tightly the materials were woven together, the stronger and more watertight the basket would be.

Women decorated their hats and baskets with zigzag patterns in honor of the mountains, which protected the Nez Perces from enemies and gave them life-sustaining waters.

32

ROUND BAGS

Women used round bags for gathering roots. Most round bags were very deep and had straps to make them easier to carry.

This unique round bag, made in the 1880s, uses wool yarn and beads for colorful accents.

CORNHUSK BAGS

Women and girls made all sizes of flat bags to carry roots and personal belongings. During Kaya's time, women used hemp and beargrass to make the bags. After corn was introduced by settlers, weavers used cornhusks, which is why the bags have the name "cornhusk bags" today.

COILED BASKETS

Flat bags were not sturdy enough for collecting easily crushed berries or holding hot water for cooking. Stiffer, stronger coiled baskets were made by stitching coils of cedar root together with beargrass and hemp.

Coyote and the Hemp Sisters

As girls worked on their basket weaving, they listened to legends like this one about how hemp came to grow in damp places. One day, Coyote met Wind at a sweat lodge. Coyote decided to play a trick on Wind, and he threw a whole basket of water on the hot stones. The water made such a great steam that Wind was scalded to death.

Coyote put on Wind's clothes. Coyote wanted the shell decorations on the clothes to rattle, so he wished for the wind to blow. Oops! His wish made Wind come back to life! The angry Wind blew Coyote to a mountaintop, where Hemp and her sister lived. Then Wind came after Coyote, but Hemp and her sister hid him over the edge of the cliff.

Coyote thanked the sisters for saving him from Wind. "How can I thank you?" he asked.

The sisters said, "There is little water here. We are thirsty all the time. We need water."

Coyote said, "I'll give you water!" Then he threw water on the rocks surrounding Hemp and her sister. And that is why hemp grows only where there is water.

Painted Parfleches

Parfleches (PAR-fleshes) are strong envelopes made of deer, elk, or buffalo rawhides. Nez Perces used them as people use suitcases and trunks today. In Kaya's time, they carried clothes, dried food, and tools. Women drew patterns onto wet hides, then filled in the patterns with bright paints. Leftover pieces of rawhide became small parfleches and bags for girls and their dolls.

Green paint was made from algae skimmed from still ponds.

Bright yellow paint could be made from lichens or gallstones from a buffalo's gallbladder.

Berries, minerals, or even pussy willow buds made many shades of red.

In modern times, women still use parfleches for storage, as decorations for their horses, and for give-aways.

Shades of blue were made from berries, crushed flowers, dark blue clay found along streams, or even duck droppings!

Bone painting tools, often made from buffalo shoulder blades or hipbones, soaked up paint and gave an even, smooth flow of color.

Sticks of willow or cottonwood with their ends frayed made stiff paintbrushes.

Willow sticks, stripped of their bark, helped artists make straight lines.

Gifts from the Land

Kaya was taught to honor nature, its creatures, and its seasons. The Nez Perces traveled with the seasons to fish, to hunt, and to gather roots and berries as they ripened. But they took only what they could eat at the time or could store for winter. To the Nez Perce, every gift from the land was sacred.

The Nez Perce Calendar

The Nez Perce divided their year according to the seasonal events that were important to their way of life.

WE-LU-POOP
The season when cold air travels

AH-LA-TAH-MAL
The season when it is difficult to build fires because fuel is scarce

LAH-TE-TAL
The season of new plants and flowers beginning to blossom

KEH-KEE-TAL
The season for the first harvest of roots

AH-PAH-AL
The season for making loaves from the kouse root

HEEL-LAL
The season of melting snow in the mountains

TOOS-TE-MA-SA-TAL
The season for traveling to the high country to dig roots

HA-SOO-AL
The season when eels run in the streams

KOY-SAL
The season when blue-back salmon run in the streams

TA-YA-AL
The season of midsummer hot weather

WA-WAMA-AYE-KHAL
The season when Chinook salmon reach the canyon streams

PE-KOON-MY-KAL
The season when the fall salmon run upstream and the fingerlings journey down the river

HOPE-LAL
The season when the tamarack trees lose their needles and trees change color

SEK-LE-WÁAL
The season when trees drop their leaves and cold comes to the high country

HA-OO-KOY
The season when new life begins in deer and elk

A Bountiful Harvest

Just as the winter stores of food were running out, the first sign of new life—the sturdy green shoots of the wild green onion plant—burst through the snow. From spring through late fall, women and children gathered all sorts of fresh new roots and berries. They celebrated the gift of renewed life and gave thanks for their great bounty.

EASY CARRYING
Women and girls gathered huckleberries, serviceberries, thimbleberries, and other berries that grew along the mountainsides. Berry baskets had loops around their rims for easy carrying.

CAMAS ROOTS
Women and girls dug bitterroots, kouse roots, onions, carrots, parsley, and many other roots and vegetables. But camas roots were a main staple of the Nez Perce diet. They could be eaten raw or baked in underground ovens.

CAMAS FIELDS
The lily-like flowers of the camas plant bloomed in June, turning the prairie into a sea of blue. After the plant finished flowering and the leaves had withered, the roots were ready for harvest.

A SOCIAL OCCASION
Thousands gathered to dig roots at camas meadows. Adults as well as children looked forward to the dancing, horse racing, feasting, and game playing.

FINGER CAKES

Women made ground kouse into a paste, which they shaped into small logs that held the shape of their fingers—finger cakes!

DIGGING STICKS

The curved shape of digging sticks made it easier to pry roots out of the ground. A girl had to learn just where to place the point of her stick. Too close, and she'd split the root. Too far, and all she'd get would be a pile of dirt!

CELEBRATE!

When the first roots or berries of the season were gathered, friends and family celebrated with feasting. They gave thanks to the Creator for these foods and honored the women who gathered them.

Kaya took pride in weaving her very own root bag.

MORTAR AND PESTLE

Women used a stone pestle to pound roots into a powder or to crush berries to make cakes. The mortar, or bowl, usually had a stone base and woven basket sides.

Sacred Salmon

During Heel-lal, when the melting snows filled the rivers and streams, the Nez Perce people watched and waited for signs that their brother, the salmon, would return. Soon the waters began to tremble with shimmering silver and red as millions of salmon made their way upstream to their spawning, or egg-laying, grounds. At the traditional fishing grounds at Celilo Falls, families gathered by the hundreds to celebrate the return of the salmon and to fish the wild waters at the base of the thunderous falls.

SALMON RUNS
The Nez Perces began fishing salmon early in the spring and followed the salmon runs until fall. They ate fresh salmon while it was available and preserved hundreds of pounds for winter storage.

Fishhooks were made from thorns or were carved out of bone and attached to hemp fishing lines.

SPEARS
Men speared fish from canoes, from platforms, and from shore. Some spears were made with the spear point attached to a rope, so a fisherman could easily retrieve it.

FISH TRAPS
In smaller streams, men used fish traps to force the fish to swim through narrow passages. Some traps were screens that caught the fish as the water passed through. Others had little trapdoors that the salmon opened as they swam upstream to spawn.

FISHNETS
Most fishing nets were made from hemp. The hemp stems were dried and shredded, then spun into twine. Men spent many long winter hours patiently knotting the twine into nets.

FISHING PLATFORMS
Nez Perce men built wooden platforms over the rapids. Men stood on the platforms and lowered long-handled nets into the stream to catch the salmon as they swam upstream against the current.

PRESERVING FISH
Women preserved fish to store for winter or to trade for other items they needed. After they split, cleaned, and sliced the fish, they hung it on poles or racks to dry in the sun.

FISH BOIL
To boil salmon and other fish, women filled baskets with water and then placed red-hot stones into the water. This made the water boil *very* quickly. Then they added the fish and let it boil until it was done.

SALMON PEMMICAN
Nez Perce women made a kind of pemmican, or nutritious dried fish mixture, by pounding dried salmon into a mush and mixing it with oil. They kneaded the mixture until it was smooth and stored it in salmon-skin bags.

SMOKED SALMON
Women cut salmon lengthwise into slices before preparing it for eating. To smoke salmon, they threaded the slices on sticks stuck in the ground around a smoky fire.

The Buffalo Hunt

In late spring and early summer, groups of Nez Perces set off on horseback to cross the Bitterroot Mountains into the plains of Buffalo Country. These hunting parties stayed away for several months or even years at a time, hunting with their friends, the Crows and Flatheads. The hunters returned with more than buffalo meat and hides. They also brought back parts of the Plains culture—feathered headdresses, beads, and rawhide cases—and adopted them as their own.

BOWS
The finest bows were made from mountain sheep horn that was heated and stretched into shape. The sinew bowstring was attached with a glue made from salmon skin.

Hunters sometimes dipped arrowheads in rattlesnake venom to make them deadlier.

ARROWS
Arrows were often made from serviceberry branches. Most arrows had several eagle or hawk feathers, which were a symbol of strength in battle.

THE BUFFALO
The Nez Perce used every bit of the buffalo, from the beard on its chin to the tip of its tail!

Hides: robes, bedding, parfleches, tepee covers, shields, clothing

BITTERROOT MOUNTAINS

Blackfeet Country

Flathead Country

Lolo Pass

Nez Perce Country

Crow Country

Horns: cups, bowls, and spoons

Brain: tanning hides

Beard: clothing decorations

GOING TO BUFFALO COUNTRY
Hunters and their families followed several ancient trails to Buffalo Country. The northern trail was very mountainous, but a shortcut known today as the Lolo Pass made this route the quickest. Still, it took a Nez Perce hunting party about two months to reach Buffalo Country. The southern route was longer but safer, because the Nez Perces were less likely to run into their enemies the Black Feet.

Buffalo rib sled

HUNTING TECHNIQUES
Hunters worked together to stalk and kill their game. Sometimes they would circle around a herd so that the animals had nowhere to run. Other times, they herded the animals over a cliff or into a stream where men in canoes waited with spears.

Buffalo tail: sweat-bath brush

Dung: fuel for fires

Bones: knives, arrows, shovels, sled runners, dice, paint tools

Buffalo hoof rattle

PREPARING MEAT
As soon as the men killed a buffalo, the women skinned and butchered it. They cooked the organs right away. They cut the meat into strips, hung them on wooden racks, and dried them in the sun.

Friends and Enemies

By Kaya's time, Nez Perces were traveling by horseback across present-day Oregon, Washington, and Idaho to visit and trade with neighboring peoples. Goods from as far away as Europe and Asia found their way into Nez Perce hands through a huge network of trading partners.

More travel also brought more conflict. Raiding parties from other bands, especially from northern neighbors such as the Blackfeet, threatened Nez Perce villages. These raiders stole horses and took captives. Often, the Nez Perces and their allies responded with raids of their own.

TRADING PARTNERS
Each year, thousands of people traveled to Celilo Falls along the Columbia River. Like Kaya, they were reunited with old friends and made new ones. Everyone looked forward to fishing, feasting, dancing, and playing games, but the main activity was trading. Along with bartering for horses, food, and hundreds of other objects, family members arranged marriages and took part in ceremonial give-aways. No one went home empty-handed!

Leather bracelet with copper inlay.

Antler horn bracelet

TO THE NORTHWEST
The Makah and Skokomish peoples traded carved bracelets, dishes filled with seal oil, dentalium shells, Chinese coins, and Russian beads.

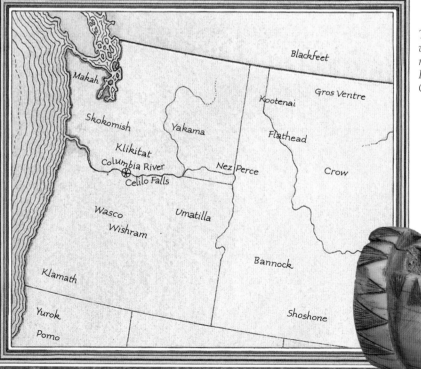

The Nez Perces had a wide trading network, ranging from the Pacific Ocean to the Great Plains.

Quail feather basket

TO THE SOUTHWEST
Acorns, elk horn purses, and quail feather baskets came from the Klamath, Yurok, and Pomo peoples.

Elk horn purse

44

Turtle bone necklace

al oil dish

Horn bowl

TO THE NORTHEAST
The people of the Plains—Flatheads, Crows, Kootenai, Gros Ventres, and Blackfeet—introduced new ornaments such as feathered headdresses, tobacco bags, necklaces made from turtle bones, and decorated buffalo robes to the Nez Perce and other tribes. They also brought buffalo meat and stone pipes to trade.

TO THE SOUTHEAST
The Shoshones and Bannocks were the first people to trade horses to the Nez Perce. They were also known for their fine arrowheads and tools carved from a glossy black stone called obsidian.

RAID!
The Nez Perces called the Shoshones and Bannocks the *Tewelka*, or "enemy to be fought." To the north, they clashed with the Blackfeet in Canada over buffalo hunting rights. Captives were often traded back to their own people at Celilo Falls. They also took advantage of opportunities to escape, just as Kaya did.

TO THE WEST
Klikitats, Wascos, Wishrams, Umatillas, and Yakamas lived nearest to Celilo Falls. They traded mountain goat skins, carved horn bowls, salmon, salmon eggs, and baskets with woven figures. The figures look much like the figures in the rock paintings along the Columbia River.

"Do Them No Hurt"

Wet-khoo-weis was a young Nez Perce girl when she was taken captive by Blackfeet warriors during a raid on her village. She was taken far from her Nez Perce homelands to Canada, where she was traded to another tribe who lived even farther to the east.

During her first years in captivity, she was traded from village to village until eventually she became the property of a kindly French Canadian. The man took her to live with him among white people in central Canada. The people there treated her with kindness and gave her medicine for her trachoma, an eye disease.

Still, Wet-khoo-weis longed for home, and she decided to escape. She wandered through the mountains until she became weak with starvation. Finally, she stumbled upon a small band of Salish, who lived just over the Bitterroot Mountains from the Nez Perce homelands. The Salish fed her and returned her to her home. The Nez Perce welcomed her back gladly and gave her the name Wet-khoo-weis, which means "returned home from a faraway place."

Many years later, the first white men came to Nez Perce country—William Clark and Meriwether Lewis. Many Nez Perces distrusted these strangers. Wet-khoo-weis was an old and dying woman, but she remembered the kindness she had received from other whites. "These are the people who helped me," she told her fellow villagers. "Do them no hurt."

Lewis and Clark

William Clark and Meriwether Lewis had been sent by President Thomas Jefferson to explore the west and find a trade route to the Pacific Ocean. The expedition had tried to cross the rugged Bitterroot Mountains too late in the season and had been caught in snow. By the time Clark and his scouts found the Nez Perce camp, they were starving and half-dead.

The people of the village and their chief, Twisted Hair, gave the starving strangers food to eat. They drew maps on elk skin to show them the river route to the sea. When the explorers were well enough to travel on, they left their horses with Twisted Hair's family for safekeeping until their return.

Lewis and Clark in the Bitterroot Mountains

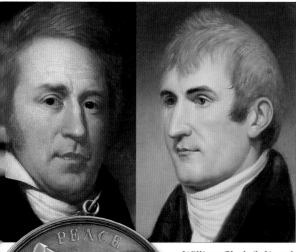

William Clark (left) and Meriwether Lewis (right)

GIFTS OF PEACE
Lewis and Clark gave Nez Perce war chiefs American flags and President Jefferson Peace and Friendship medals.

TAKING NOTES
Members of the Lewis and Clark expedition kept detailed notes of their explorations. One member of the party wrote about the Nez Perces, "All the Indians from the Rocky Mountains to the falls of Columbia are an honest, ingenuous, and well-disposed people."

I am taken verry unwell with a paine in the bowels & Stomach, which is certainly the effects of my diet.

STRANGE FOODS, SAVING FOODS
The dried salmon and camas-root cakes that the Nez Perce gave the explorers probably saved their lives. But the white men were not used to Nez Perce food.

RIDING THE RAPIDS
The Nez Perce helped Lewis and Clark make sturdy dugout canoes by burning out the centers of large tree trunks. Today, you can see one of these canoes at the Nez Perce National Historic Park in Spalding, Idaho.

More Strangers from Afar

The Nez Perces were very interested in Lewis and Clark's journals, and they wanted to find out more about reading and writing. In 1831, four Nez Perce men traveled to St. Louis, Missouri. They met with their old friend, William Clark, who had become Commissioner of Indian Affairs, and asked for books and teachers.

In 1836, Henry and Eliza Spalding arrived in Nez Perce country. The Spaldings were missionaries, who traveled to teach about Christianity. They would teach the Nez Perces to read and write in English, too.

HENRY SPALDING
Henry Spalding wanted his Nez Perce followers to give up their traditional beliefs and become farmers. Many Nez Perces believed that the earth was their mother and that plowing would cut and wound her. Those who refused to take up the whites' ways were punished by whipping.

THE PRINTED WORD
Missionaries were the first to record the Nez Perce language in writing. They imported a printing press from Hawaii and published several books, including the New Testament and a list of laws, in the Nez Perce language.

"LADDER TO HEAVEN AND HELL"
Since the Spaldings had difficulty learning to speak Nez Perce, they used pictures to help the Nez Perces understand Christianity. This illustration by Eliza Spalding shows the paths to Heaven and Hell.

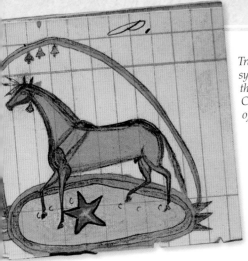

Traditional Nez Perce beliefs are symbolized in this drawing from the 1880s. Some Nez Perces viewed Christianity as yet another source of spiritual strength.

"CIVILIZATION"
Missionaries encouraged white pioneers to settle on Nez Perce homelands and help "civilize" the area. The settlers plowed ancient food-gathering lands and brought diseases that killed native peoples by the thousands.

Gold!

By the 1850s, settlers and gold miners were swarming onto Nez Perce lands. In 1855, the U.S. government offered the Nez Perces a treaty. The treaty set aside land called a reservation for the Nez Perce people alone.

Then, just eight years later, gold was discovered on the Nez Perce reservation land, and the government changed the treaty. The new treaty took away all but about one-tenth of the Nez Perce lands. Fearing war, some of the Nez Perce bands agreed to the new treaty. Others refused to sign. Those who refused were called the "non-treaty" Indians.

Gold nuggets

In 1877, the government told the non-treaty Nez Perces that they had to move to the reservation or face war. The chiefs knew that their little bands couldn't win against the Americans. Sadly, they began the long, slow journey to the reservation. On the way there, a group of angry young Nez Perces raided some white settlements. More than a dozen settlers were killed or wounded. To the government, the raids were a declaration of war. The chiefs still hoped to negotiate peace, but the army attacked before they could speak. The Nez Perce War had begun.

THE SPLIT
Some Nez Perce people adopted white ways. They gave up their buckskin clothing, cut their hair short, and became farmers. The split between the two groups—those who followed white ways and those who followed Indian ways—destroyed the unity of the Nez Perce.

49

Fleeing to Safety

After the raids, the Nez Perce chiefs knew their people would have to flee to survive. They led about 800 Nez Perces, starting from Wallowa Valley and traveling along the Lolo Pass through the Bitterroot Mountains. They hoped to find help and safety with their friends the Crows in Montana. It was a desperate journey, with U.S. soldiers chasing them the whole way.

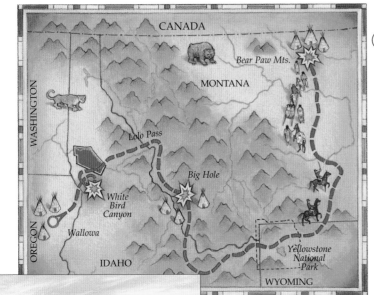

CANADA
Bear Paw Mts.
MONTANA
WASHINGTON
Lolo Pass
Big Hole
White Bird Canyon
OREGON
Wallowa
IDAHO
Yellowstone National Park
WYOMING

④ **RALLYING THE PEOPLE**
When the Nez Perces reached Big Hole, a valley in Montana, they were badly in need of a rest. On the second afternoon of their stay, warriors paraded to show their pride and strength.

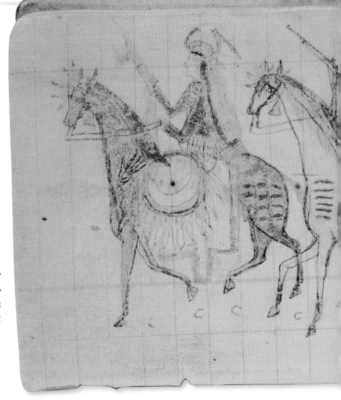

The warriors' horses have honor marks painted on their flanks.

① **THE PATH OF WAR**
Before the Nez Perce War was finished, U.S. army soldiers chased the Nez Perces for more than a thousand miles.

⑤ **STANDING STRONG**
The women watched the parade dressed in their finest clothes. Women did much more than watch parades, however. Without their speed in moving the camp, many more Nez Perce lives would have been lost. And when their men were killed, women stepped in to continue the fight.

② **KEEP MOVING**
While the soldiers had to move only themselves, the Nez Perces had to move their entire community. Men, women, children, and elders had to keep moving and stay together.

③ **ONE STEP AHEAD**
Nez Perce warriors captured as many of the soldiers' horses as they could. The halters on these horses drawn by an unknown Nez Perce man show that they were taken from whites.

The woman in front may have scars on her arm, a sign of grief after losing a loved one.

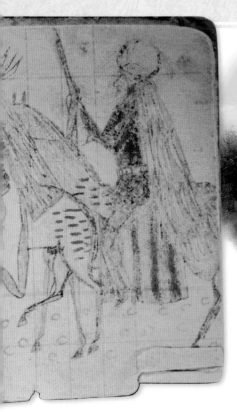

⑥ THE BATTLE AT BIG HOLE

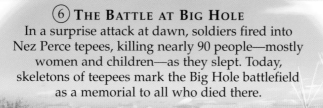

In a surprise attack at dawn, soldiers fired into Nez Perce tepees, killing nearly 90 people—mostly women and children—as they slept. Today, skeletons of teepees mark the Big Hole battlefield as a memorial to all who died there.

⑦ FRIENDS IN NEED

When the Nez Perces reached the Crows, their friends would not help them. The Nez Perces traveled on to Canada to find the Sioux chief Sitting Bull. His people lived in exile—and safety—after defeating U.S. troops.

Chief Sitting Bull

⑧ LAST HOPE

At the Bear Paw Mountains, the U.S. soldiers attacked for the last time. A handful of Nez Perce scouts rode to Sitting Bull and asked for his help. By the time the Sioux arrived, it was too late.

Surrender

After five days of fighting, the army colonel promised the Nez Perces that they could keep their horses and return to Idaho if they would surrender. With that promise, Chief Joseph said these words:

Tell General Howard that I know his heart. What he told me before, I have it in my heart. I am tired of fighting…. It is cold, and we have no blankets. The little children are freezing to death. My people, some of them, have run away to the hills, and have no blankets, no food. No one knows where they are—perhaps freezing to death. I want to have time to look for my children, and see how many of them I can find. Maybe I shall find them among the dead. Hear me, my chiefs! I am tired. My heart is sick and sad. From where the sun now stands, I will fight no more forever.

The colonel had promised the Nez Perces that they would return to Idaho. Instead, men, women, children, and elders were sent as prisoners of war to a camp in Kansas. Many died of malaria and other diseases. Almost twenty years later, they were allowed to return to the Northwest, but they never lived in their homelands again.

Different hairstyles show that warriors to the left of the drum are Sioux, and those to the right are Nez Perce.

A Strong and Proud Heritage

The Nez Perce people have lost much over the past 200 years, but they have never lost their spirit. The Nez Perce War scattered the people to different reservations and all over the world, breaking bonds that had been built over generations. Yet, as the Nez Perce saying goes, "Wherever we go, we are always Nez Perce." The Nez Perce people have worked hard to keep their culture alive and strong no matter where they lived, and they have succeeded. Nez Perce children continue to hear the legends and learn the songs, dances, and arts of their people. They proudly carry on the traditions of their ancestors, and one day they will pass them on to their own children.

CARING FOR HORSES
Horses are still a prized, and much-loved, part of Nez Perce culture. This girl and her family are members of the Nez Perce Appaloosa Horse Club. The club's horse clinics teach people of all ages about Appaloosa history, as well as how to care for and ride these fine horses. Other Nez Perce groups, such as the Young Horsemen Project and the Mounted Scholars Program, also offer the opportunity to bond with and learn from horses.

RETURN TO THE HOMELAND
Chief Joseph was never allowed to live again in his beloved Wallowa Valley. But today, his descendants can—and do—return each year for a celebration called *Tamkaliks,* "Where You Can See the Mountains." The celebration begins with a horseback procession, symbolizing the Nez Perces' return to their Wallowa homelands.

KEEPING THE LANGUAGE
As more and more Nez Perce children grew up in the midst of white culture, the Nez Perce language slowly started to slip away. In 1996, tribal elders began teaching classes for adults and children. Today, classes are even offered at the college level at Lewis-Clark State College in Idaho.

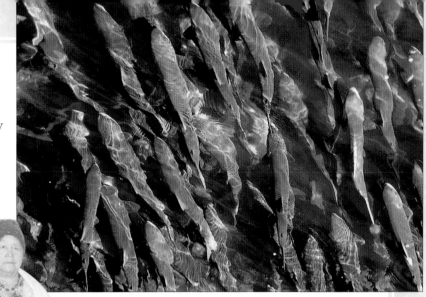

HELPING A BROTHER

The Nez Perce tribe is working toward the day when the wolf will no longer be on the endangered species list. In 1995, 35 gray wolves were brought from Canada to Idaho. The Nez Perce tribe was entrusted with their care, and today more than 250 gray wolves live in Idaho.

SAVING THE SALMON

Millions of salmon swam in the streams in Kaya's day, while only a few thousand survive today. Eight federal dams have been built between the streams where the salmon are born and the ocean where they live as adults. The Nez Perce, along with other tribes, are working to have four dams partially removed to help the salmon return to the streams.

Nez Perce families still have wedding give-aways today. The groom's and bride's families exchange gifts packed in parfleches or, for a more modern twist, wrapped in handmade quilts.

SEE IT FOR YOURSELF

One of the best places to learn about Nez Perce culture is the Visitors' Center at the Nez Perce National Historical Park, located in Spalding, Idaho. Visitors from all over the world come to look at Nez Perce clothing, horse gear, and other artifacts from long ago and today.

CULTURE CAMP

Each summer, Nez Perce girls and boys can attend Culture Camp to learn from their elders such traditional skills as beading, basket weaving, making traditional foods, building tepees, dancing, and much more.

Pow-wow!

One of the most exciting and beautiful celebrations of Indian culture is the pow-wow. Today's Nez Perce girls love dancing at pow-wows for many reasons. They love the feeling of pride it gives them—pride in their ancestors and their culture as well as in their own dancing. They love seeing the colorful outfits and accessories, or regalia, and feeling the beat of the drums. But mostly they love dancing for the same reason all girls love dancing—because it's fun!

JINGLE DANCERS
The jingle dress dance was originally an Ojibway dance, but it is now danced by people from many tribes. The dresses are decorated with rows and rows of tinkling metal cones. Jingle dancers hold their hands on their hips and step light and lively, making the cones sing along with the drumbeats.

THE GRAND ENTRY
Most pow-wows begin with a Grand Entry. Everyone stands as the eagle staff and other flags are carried into the arena. Next, elders and other important guests are honored. Finally, in a grand flash of color and movement, the dancers arrive dressed in full regalia. The Grand Entry ends with a prayer of thanks for the gathering.

TRADITIONAL STYLE
Girls and women compete in the traditional, fancy shawl, and jingle styles of dancing. Traditional dancers wear belted buckskin or cloth dresses. When they dance, they move with dignity and grace, heads held high and backs kept straight, while they gently step to the beat of the drum.

Traditional dancers waiting to dance

SACRED DRUMMING
People say that those who take part in pow-wows "follow the drum." Its beat is the heartbeat of the earth, the mother of all people.

54

FANCY SHAWL DANCERS

Girl fancy shawl dancers wear colorful shawls spread over their shoulders. When they hold onto the shawls' edges, it looks as if the dancers have wings as they dip and swoop and soar with quick, light steps.

WHIPWOMAN

One elder woman, called the Whipwoman, is in charge of all the female dancers. She carries a special staff—but it's for leading dances, not for whipping!

As these young boys dance, they dip and bob their heads like quail.

TEPEE CAMPS

Camping out is part of the fun of pow-wows. Some people set up tepees in the "old ways" of their ancestors.

Men dance in the fancy style, too. They wear outfits decorated with lots of feathers, ribbons, and fringe. When they dance, they spin so fast that they become blurs of bright color.

FRIENDSHIP DANCE

Everyone is invited to join in friendship dances. The dancers form an inner ring and an outer ring, and they shake hands with everyone they meet as they slowly dance around the circle.

A Peek into the Future

From the book *Changes for Kaya*

"You'll need much strength in the days ahead if you're to work as your namesake did to feed the people. Now it is time for you to wear this." Kautsa placed the hat firmly on Kaya's head.

"I'm ready, Kautsa," Kaya said.

—Janet Shaw,
Changes for Kaya

Kaya's world in 1764 was not very different from the world her ancestors had known for thousands of years. How could Kaya have known that by the time her own grandchildren were grown, her world, and the world of her ancestors, would be changed forever?

Perhaps Kaya would have sensed the winds of change. She would have been an elder herself when Lewis and Clark reached the Nez Perce homelands. Maybe she, like Wet-khoo-weis, would have counseled her people to do the strangers no harm. Or maybe, like others, she would have heeded dreams that foretold danger.

As an elder, Kaya would have taught her grand-children that they were part of the earth. But her grandchildren were to see most of their sacred lands taken away from them. Her great-grandchildren were to be punished in school for speaking the language and practicing the traditions that she and other elders had passed along.

If Kaya were to meet her own people today, how-ever, she would be filled with renewed hope and pride. Much would surprise her. She'd meet artists, computer engineers, scientists, students attending colleges, and children playing on basketball teams. She would also see children learning the Nez Perce language again, and storytellers passing along the same legends she had told her own grandchildren. She'd see young girls learning traditional dances and raising horses that look just like Steps High. She'd see her people working to return the salmon and wolves to their homes and to restore the balance between their mother earth and her children.

Kaya would know that the wisdom that she passed down to her grandchildren—the strength and spirit of Nimíipuu—would survive.